Is 2012 The End Of The World?

CURRICULUM FOR YOUTH
A FAITH OUT LOUD MODULE

Discipleship Ministry Team
Ministry Council
Cumberland Presbyterian Church

Fall 2012

8207 Traditional Place
Cordova (Memphis), Tennessee 38016

The Discipleship Ministry Team of the Ministry Council of the Cumberland Presbyterian Church is the successor organization to the Board of Christian Education of the Cumberland Presbyterian Church.

Funded, in part, by your contributions to Our United Outreach.

First Edition 2012

Published by The Discipleship Ministry Team, CPC
Memphis, Tennessee

ISBN-13: 978-0615684437
ISBN-10: 0615684432

Reverse: Bengt Ekerot as Death from the 1957 film *The Seventh Seal*. ©1958 Janus Films.

We want to hear from you.
Please send your comments about this curriculum to
the Discipleship Ministry Team at faithoutloud@cumberland.org

OUR UNITED OUTREACH
Made Possible In Part By Your Tithe To Our United Outreach

Welcome to the *Faith Out Loud* curriculum!

We're excited to release this curriculum to equip you to guide and educate your students towards a deeper faith in Christ and a growing understanding of the beliefs we hold as Cumberland Presbyterians. The series author, Dr. Andy McClung, has created engaging lessons that help students begin to think deeply and critically about their Christian beliefs and offers them practical ways to live out their faith daily.

It is our prayer that these lessons both encourage you and equip you as a youth leader—we're so grateful for what you do in the lives of students!

Blessings to you and your ministry!

The following guide explains the components found in each lesson and offers tips to get the most out of this curriculum.

- **Lesson Title**: Each lesson has a catchy title. Use these titles as teasers to get your students excited about upcoming gatherings.
- **Scripture**: Each lesson has a key scripture reference. Spend some time studying and praying through each week's passage as you prepare to teach.
- **Theme**: The theme statement gives you a quick snapshot into the main point of the lesson.
- **Before The Lesson**: This section is usually divided into two sections: *Supplies* and *Preparations*. *Supplies* give you a quick list of all the stuff you need to gather for each week. *Preparations* give detailed instructions on the advance work that needs to be done for that week's activities. Do NOT wait until the night before you teach to review this section.
- **The Lesson**: Once you move into the teaching time, you'll see these recurring elements:
  - **Opening Activity:** These activities are designed to draw students into the material and set up the theme for the lesson.
  - **Discussion Questions:** Usually a group of open-ended questions, these moments in the lesson are strategically placed to encourage your students to both think about and respond to the topic at hand.
  - **Explain:** Placed in italics, these sections can be read verbatim to your students to help them fully understand the implications of the topic or

theme. You'll discover you'll get the best response when you are thoroughly familiar with these sections and can deliver the same information in your own words instead of just reading the info to the students.

- o **Leader Note:** You'll find sections of blue text throughout each lesson. These are notes just for you, the leader. These notes offer you everything from instructions on how to facilitate the activities to background information on the subject to tips in making your lesson run smoothly.
- o **Read:** This section highlights a key scripture passage that should be read aloud. Encourage student to do these readings as often as possible.
- o **Parting Ways:** This is simply just the closing of each lesson, designed to help you end your time with your students well and offer them something to think about in the week ahead. Most weeks have handouts to pass along to your students during this time. You may find it helpful to encourage your students to get a folder to keep these handouts together so they can easily refer to them during the week.
- **Just In Case:** Found after the teaching portion of the lesson, this section offers you as the leader some additional insights into related topics your students may bring up or enrichment that can enhance your understanding of the material.
- **Handouts:** At the end of each week's lesson, you'll find a reproducible page. Your purchase of this curriculum grants you the right to print and distribute copies to everyone in your group.

Is 2012 the End?

by Andy McClung

Scripture: Matthew 24:36

Theme: People are saying the world will end on December 21, 2012. Where does this idea come from, and what is a Christian to think about it?

Resource List

- Computer or DVD player
- Projector
- Internet and video capability
- Speakers
- Clip from the movie *Big Fish*
- Clip from the movie *2012*

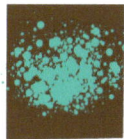

Leader Prep

- Prepare for viewing the scene from the movie *Big Fish* in Chapter 2 of the DVD, 10:08 to 13:26. You can also find it at http://www.youtube.com/watch?v=41J45SvosV0&feature=related. Please cue this clip to 00:30 to avoid any curse words. End the clip at 7:23. Preview the clip before showing to your class.
- Prepare the YouTube video clip "Watch a 5 Minute clip from 2012 - on Blu-ray & DVD." It can be found at http://www.youtube.com/watch?v=H50jTU4vqA0 or "2012 Trailer #2" which can be found at http://www.youtube.com/watch?v=ceON3TEcFw0.

Leader Insight

Connecting to Your Students

Your students have undoubtedly heard about the predictions that the world will end on December 21, 2012. Teens are still developing the ability to think beyond the immediate future, but they are probably interested in this subject. They may have seen some of the movies about it, whether the big-budget Hollywood productions or the smaller-budget films. They may have seen some of the TV specials, whether science-based or propaganda-based.

It is likely that your students will present an apathetic face toward such potential dangers, but at some level they are concerned about the end of the world. They are old enough not to believe adults who say, "Don't worry; everything's going to be all right" without being offered some evidence to back up that assurance. Use this lesson to offer students a safe, non-judgmental place to voice any fears they have about this issue.

Explaining the Lesson

The idea that the world will end December 21, 2012, is based on a calendar that the ancient Mayans developed, but they didn't circle that day and write, "World ends." Pseudo-scientists have added that part, either after making unfounded assumptions or after bending the Mayan stuff to match what they already believed.

We think of the progression of years as linear: we move up a grade each year in school; we note sequential anniversaries of important days; we add "1" to the year every January first. The Mayans didn't think about time in such a linear fashion; they thought of time as running in cycles, kind of like how we view the seasons. To a farmer it doesn't really matter what year it is. What matters is that it's spring and time for planting, so the harvest will be ready by fall.

The Mayan culture thrived in and around the Yucatan Peninsula (Guatemala and southern Mexico) from about 2,000 B.C. to A.D. 250, possibly reaching a population as high as 20 million. Archeologists tell us that the Mayans were advanced, slightly ahead of most of the world at the time: developing a written language, designing and building cities with large and precisely-placed structures, using advanced mathematics, having a remarkable understanding of astronomy, but, oddly, not wheels or beasts of burden. By A.D. 900 the major Mayan cities had been abandoned. We don't know why, but speculations abound. The Spanish conquest of the area in the 1500s and 1600s destroyed most records, along with almost everybody who could interpret the few records left.

In light of this lesson, a most interesting fact about the Mayans is that they developed a calendar based on the movement of the stars. It measured 13 cycles of 144,000 days each, which totals 5,125 years. This is called the Long Count Calendar. It started on August 11, 3114 B.C., which was before the Mayans were even around. It's unknown why they started the calendar there; again, speculations abound. Cycle 13, the final cycle, of this calendar ends on December 21, 2012, if archeologists have correctly translated the few clues about understanding this calendar.

The Mayans never predicted anything other than the movement of the sun, stars, planets, and moon. Translating Mayan writings is a highly subjective endeavor, and some researchers have drawn a connection between the 2012 date and a supposed alignment between the sun, the earth, and the center of our galaxy—something that happens every 26,000 years or so. Put all this together, add a bit of imagination, and the result is that the Mayans "predicted" that on December 21, 2012, this alignment of heavenly bodies would occur, causing cataclysmic natural disasters and the end of the world.

Other cultures also have or had stories about the end of the world, including the Egyptians, the Hopi Indians, Buddhists, the Vikings, and Christians. The problem with stating a specific day, however, is that people have been saying such things for…well…always. People have always thought the world was going to end soon. Some have put an exact date on the end, and they have all been wrong. The most recent person to predict the end of the world was Harold Camping. He spent millions trying to convince everyone, and actually convinced thousands, that he had used scripture to determine that the world would end on May 21, 2011. When that day came and went and the world was still here, Camping said he'd made a miscalculation and the real date was October 21. That day, too, has come and gone. So have the 1988 and 1994 dates he predicted.

Camping is not alone. Many people have made such predictions. Hal Lindsey said the world would end by the year 2000, and before that he said we would all be gone before the 1980s were over. Benjamin Keach, a Baptist preacher, said it would be in 1689. Thomas Brightman, a Presbyterian, also thought it would happen in the late 1600s. William Miller, another Baptist preacher, said it would be March 21, 1843,…and then April 18, 1844. Since 1915, the Jehovah's Witnesses have set nine different dates, all of which have passed.

NASA says that the sun, earth, and the galaxy's center may indeed align sometime soon, but there's no way to pinpoint the exact year, much less the exact day. NASA also says there's no reason to think that this alignment will have any more effect on earth than the planetary alignments over the past few decades. People said those alignments would do all sorts of things, but they came and went with no effects on earth.

Leader Tip:
The stars and the sun, of course, don't actually move. They just look like they do because the earth is moving.

Notes:

Theological Underpinnings

The prophets of the Bible primarily spoke for God to the people about their present situation, but they sometimes spoke about future events, too. But they never offered any exact or even approximate dates for things that would happen in the future. Jesus also spoke of things to come. When Jesus spoke of the end of the world, he was decidedly vague. Once, after explaining some of the signs that would precede the day of his second coming, which is generally understood to precede the end of the world, Jesus said, "But about that day and hour no one knows, neither the angels of heaven, nor the Son, but only the Father" (Matthew 24:36).

So, anyone who says he or she knows when Jesus will return or when the world will end is claiming to know what only God knows. That's pretty arrogant. That's wanting and trying to be like God in power and knowledge rather than trying to be like God in character, which was the first sin humans committed. (See FAITH OUT LOUD, Volume 2, Quarter 1, Lesson 1, "The Fall.") Wanting and trying to be like God is the very thing that caused us to lose the perfect relationship with God, creation, and one another that God intended for us.

The opening activities should get students thinking about the end of the world, or at least the end of their own world. "Listen Up" should calm any fears about December 12. The activities in "Now What?" and "Live" affirm that life is indeed finite, and points to Jesus as the source of peace in this life and as the hope for life beyond this life.

Applying the Lesson to Your Own Life

Think back to the hysteria around the end of 1999. Not just the Y2K computer scare, but all the people saying the world would end with the new millennium. How did you react to such claims? Have you been aware of the predictions about December 21, 2012? How have you been reacting to them?

In the past there seemed to be an overarching fear for each new generation: communism, nuclear war, AIDS, random violence. Today we're dealing with multiple overarching fears all at once: random violence, global economic collapse, end of the world. How many of these fears have you seen come and go over the years? How many more do you think you'll see come and go in your lifetime? Amid all these fears, has anything steadily remained as a source of hope and peace for you?

Get Started (12 min.)

Video: Big Fish

Show students a scene from the movie *Big Fish*.

Warning: *In this scene a cuss word is spelled and briefly a man is shown sitting on a toilet with no nudity. If such things are offensive, skip the video and give the following verbal summary.*

In a scene from the movie *Big Fish*, a group of children sneak through the woods to visit an old lady whom they think is a witch. The rumor around town is that if you look into her glass eye you'll see how you're going to die. Some of the children chicken out and run way before even meeting the witch. Three boys remain, but only Edward is brave enough to ask the witch about her eye. The other two boys look into it. One sees himself dying as an old man and gets a little scared. The other boy sees himself dying as a young man and gets very scared. Edward says to the witch, "I was thinking about death and all. About seeing how you're going to die. I mean, on one hand, if dying was all you thought about, it could kind of screw you up. But it could kind of help you, couldn't it? Because you'd know that everything else you can survive." Edward looks into the eye, smiles, and accepts his fate with peace. Many years later as he lies in what everyone believes to be his death bed, Edward tells his adult son, with utter peace, "People needn't worry so much. It's not my time yet. This is not how I go. I saw it in the eye."

Discussion Questions:
- Would it be better to know when and how you're going to die, or would it be better to be surprised?
- Would it be better for humankind to know when and how the world will end, or would it be better for humankind to be surprised?
- What would you do if you knew the world would end in one month?

Say: *Lots of people have wondered what the end of the world will be like. There have been many movies about it. Just a few years ago, a lot of people were worried that the world would end in the year 2000.*

Listen Up (20 min.)

Share with your students what you remember about the hysteria surrounding 1999 becoming 2000. Not just the Y2K computer scare, but the predictions about the world ending, or at least the threat of it becoming mostly destroyed. You may want to list some of the top-grossing movies that came out around then:

- *Independence Day* (1996)—aliens try to take over the world and destroy much of it in the attempt.
- *Twister* (1996)—tornadoes destroy a lot of stuff in Oklahoma.
- *The Fifth Element* (1997)—aliens are heading for earth to destroy it.
- *Volcano* (1997)—a volcano erupts and destroys much of Los Angeles.
- *Dante's Peak* (1997)—a volcano erupts and destroys a town.
- *Starship Troopers* (1997)—aliens attack earth.
- *Deep Impact* (1998)—a comet threatens to destroy Earth.
- *Armageddon* (1998) in which an asteroid threatens to destroy earth.
- *Lost in Space* (1998)—the earth has been rendered uninhabitable due to pollution and global warming.
- *The Matrix* (1999)—a computer secretly has taken over the earth.
- *End of Days* (1999)—the devil, on the eve of the new millennium, comes to earth to destroy it.

Discussion Question:
- What, if anything, do these movies have in common?

Note that from 2000 to 2002, after people knew that the new millennium wasn't going to bring disaster, none of the top-grossing movies dealt with the end of the world or widespread destruction. The next big disaster movie, *The Core*, didn't come out until 2003.

Ask how many of your students have seen the movie *2012*, which was released in 2009.

Show the YouTube clip entitled "Watch a 5 Minute clip from 2012 - on Blu-ray & DVD." Warning: this clip contains scenes of natural disaster and lots of people dying, but no gore. If that's too much for your class, show a trailer for the movie instead, maybe "2012 Trailer #2."

Discussion Questions:
- Does anybody think that's really going to happen before this year is over?
- If you have mostly negative answers: Is anybody a little worried that something like that might happen?
- What have you heard about the end of the world prediction for December 21?

Allow responses, and explain as much as you think is pertinent from the background material in "Explaining the Lesson." This part of the lesson will work much better as a conversation than a lecture, and the more casual the better. That means this part of the lesson may be harder to plan, as your students may have bits and pieces of factual information mixed in with some speculation, theories, and outright craziness. Try to be familiar enough with the background information to respond to the non-scientific stuff as it comes up, consulting your notes as infrequently as possible.

As students discuss, try some of these questions and comments if you need to deepen the conversation:
- Say a little more about that.
- What do most teenagers think about that? What do you think about it?
- How do most teenagers feel concerning that? How do you feel about it?
- Where is God in this?
- Where is the church in this?

You'll have to transition from conversation partner back into teacher to move from this part of the lesson to the next. If it hasn't come up already, this is a good time to assure your students that what's being presented as fact by some really isn't fact, and that many of the claims about what the Mayans said are really just people projecting their own ideas onto flimsy evidence.

Conclude this portion of the lesson with:
- As advanced as the Mayans were, and as long as they were around, their civilization pretty much disappeared over 1,000 years ago. We see this same thing happen throughout history: every civilization, every culture, no matter how great, comes to an end sooner or later. How long do you think the U.S. (Europe, Africa, Japan,

Leader Tip:
Leading this part of the lesson in a casual manner will open the door for students to be more forthright with their feelings, fears, concerns, and questions about the end-of-the-world predictions.

Leader Tip:
Even though we've studied the Mayans for several decades, the end of their calendar being associated with the end of the world only started in 1975. The idea was so unscientific that no one paid any attention to it until 1987 when somebody put it together with false data about planetary alignment. Even then, no one took it seriously until 1995 when the idea was coupled with more faulty data about heavenly alignment. Since then, though, the idea has grown in popularity.

or another countryor continent) will be around?

- The best guess is that a combination of factors wiped out the Mayans: overpopulation, depletion of natural resources, warfare, and a lack of preventative actions by leaders. What do you think might cause our civilization to collapse?
- If the U.S. disappears, how do you think that will affect Christianity?

Allow responses to this final question, but assure your students that the Christian Church is far bigger than the U.S. In fact, experts now tell us that the church is growing far faster outside the U.S. than within, especially in Central America and Africa.

Now What? (15 min.)

Say something like: *The world probably isn't going to end when humans predict it, but we never know when a natural disaster might happen. It's a good idea to be prepared by having a family plan, an emergency kit, first-aid supplies, and food and water. None of us are probably going to die anytime soon, either, but it's a good idea to be ready for that as well. We prepare ourselves for death by entrusting our lives to God through Christ.*

Then say: *Part of being prepared for a disaster is thinking ahead, having a plan. So let's spend a few minutes thinking about what each of us would do in an earthquake, flood, hurricane, tornado, tsunami, or something else that wipes out power and communication, and overburdens emergency services.*

Explain that you will read off eight choices. Students have to select one of the choices you mention and group themselves according to their choices. No sitting on the fence, making up another option, or choosing none of the above.

The choices are:
1. Stay put and pray for somebody to rescue you.
2. Search for survivors whom you might be able to help.
3. Do whatever it takes to keep other people away from the food and water you've stashed away for yourself

and your family.

4. Do whatever it takes to get food and water from somebody else.
5. Follow the plan you've made with your family and neighbors to share resources and help one another.
6. Hope to die within the first few minutes of the disaster so that you don't have to deal with the situation.
7. Let your parents worry about this. It's their job to make sure you're safe.
8. Don't plan to do anything because nothing like this will ever happen.

Once all students have made their choices and formed groups based on their answers, ask a few to explain their choices—one from each group, if you have time. Ask if anyone wants to change his or her group based on the responses.

Live It (5 min.)

Say: As Christians, we have our own story about how the world will end. It's called Armageddon and is found in the Book of Revelation. If you had to sum up Revelation using only one word, that word would have to be: weird. You could spend the rest of your life trying to figure out what Revelation means and still only have guesses. If Revelation really is an accurate vision of "the end," then the only really important thing to know is that Christ wins.

Say it again: Christ wins.

Say: No matter when the world ends, no matter how the world ends, no matter when or how we die…if we're on Christ' side, we're on the winning side.

Close your time together in prayer.

Resources used: Collapse, by Jared Diamond; Huffington-post.com; nasa.gov; The New American Desk Encyclopedia; The Westminster Guide to the Books of the Bible.

Notes:

The End of the World in Popular Culture

A list of "End of the World" centered books, television programs, and movies follows. You might find some of these items useful particularly if you choose to expand this module beyond a single lesson. Keep in mind, however, that as soon as a list like this is compiled, it is out of date. Be ready for one of your students to exclaim, *"What about. . ."* and name a book or video that is not on this list.

Movies

20 Years After
2012
2019, After The Fall Of New York
28 Days Later
A Boy and his Dog
A Wind Named Amnesia
Aftermath, The (Zombie Aftermath)
Bed Sitting Room, The
Blindness
Book of Eli, The
Captive Women
Children Of Men
City Of Lost Children, The (La Cite Des Enfants Perdus)
Damnation Alley
Day After, The
Day After Tomorrow, The
Day Of The Triffids, The
Day The World Ended, The
Death Of Grass, The
DefCon 4
Deluge
Doom Runners
Doomsday
End Of The World (Panic In Year Zero)
End Of The World (La Fin du Monde)
Fail Safe
Final War, The (1960)
Final War, The (1962)
Fire Next Time, The
Five
I Am Legend
In The Year 2889
Last Battle, The (Le Dernier Combat)
Last Man, The (Le Dernier Homme) (1968)
Last Man, The (2000)
Last Man on Earth, The

Last Woman On Earth, The
Mad Max
Mad Max II
Mad Max III – Beyond Thunderdome
Malevil
Miracle Mile
Night Of The Comet
No Blade Of Grass
Omega Man, The
On The Beach (1959)
On The Beach (2000)
Panic In Year Zero
Postman, The
Quiet Earth, The
Right At Your Door
Road, The
Tank Girl
Testament
Threads
War Game, The
Waterworld
When The Wind Blows
When Worlds Collide
World, the Flesh, and the Devil, The
Where Have All The People Gone?

Television

Day of the Triffids, The (1981)
Day of the Triffids, The (2009)
Dead Set
Jeremiah
Jericho
Last Train, The
Offshore Island, The
Stand, The
Survivors (1975 – 1977)
Survivors (2008 – 2010)

Tribe, The
Walking Dead, The
Woops!
Z For Zachariah

Books

A Boy and His Dog (by Harlan Ellison)
A Canticle for Leibowitz (by Walter Miller)
A Gift Upon the Shore (by M K Wren)
A Messiah at the End of Time (by Michael Moorcock)
A World For The Meek (by Harry Willson)
A Wrinkle In The Skin (by John Christopher)
After London (by Richard Jefferies)
After The Fire (Series) (by John Lockley)
After The Plague (by Jean Ure)
After Worlds Collide (by Edwin Balmer & Philip Wylie)
Against Nature (by John Nelson)
Air Battle: A Vision Of The Future, The
Alas Babylon (by Pat Frank)
All Fools Day (by Edmund Cooper)
Among The Hidden (Series) (by Margaret Peterson Haddix)
Armageddon Summer (by Jane Yolen and Bruce Coville)
Ashes Ashes (by Rene Barjavel)
Ashes (Series) (by William W Johnstone)
Battle Circle Trilogy (by Piers Anthony)
Battlefield Earth (by L Ron Hubbard)
Bewitchments of Love and Hate, The (by Storm Constantine)
Blessing Trilogy, The (by William Barnwell)
Blood Crazy (by Simon Clark)
Book of the New Sun, The (by Gene Wolfe)
Burning World, The (by J G Ballard)
Brave New World (by Aldous Huxley)
Brief History of the Dead, The (by Kevin Brockmeier)
Brother in the Land (by Robert Swindells)
By the Waters of Babylon (by Stephen Vincent Benet)
C.A.D.S (Series), The (by Ryder Syvertsen/David Alexander)
Casca (Series), The (by Barry Sadler)
Castle Keeps, The (by Andrew J Offutt)
Cat's Cradle (by Kurt Vonnegut)

Children of the Dust (by Louise Lawrence)
Childhood's End (by Arthur C Clark)
Chrysalids, The (by John Wyndham)
City Of Embers (Series) (by Jeanne Duprau)
Collapse of Homo Sapiens, The (by P Anderson Graham)
Crystal World, The (by J G Ballard)
Damnation Alley (by Roger Zelazny)
Dark December (by Edmund Cooper)
Darkness and Dawn (by George Allan England)
Darwath Trilogy (by Barbara Hambly)
Dawn (by S Fowler Wright)
Dawn's Uncertain Light (by Neal Barrett Jnr)
Day of the Triffids, The (by John Wyndham)
Death is a Dream (by Edwin Charles Tubb)
Deathland Series (by James Axler)
Death of Grass, The (by John Christopher)
Defender (Series) (by Jerry Ahern)
Deluge (by S Fowler Wright)
Destiny's Road (by Larry Niven)
Dies The Fire (by S M Stirling)
Doomsday Warrior (Series) (by Ryder Syvertsen)
Dr. Bloodmoney (by Philip K Dick)
Dream Millenium, The (by James White)
Drought, The (by J G Ballard)
Drowned World, The (by J G Ballard)
Earth Abides (by George R Stewart)
Earthblood Series (by James Axler)
Emergence (by David Palmer)
Empty World (by John Christopher)
Enchantments of Flesh and Spirit, The (by Storm Constantine)
End of all Songs, The (by Michael Moorcock)
Ende: A Diary Of The Third World War (by Andon-Andreas Guha)
Endgame (play by Samuel Beckett)
Endworld (Series) (by David L Robbins)
Eternity Road (by Jack McDevitt)
False Dawn (by Chelsea Quinn Yarbro)
Famine (by Graham Masterton)
Faraday's Orphans (by N Lee Wood)
Farnham's Freehold (by Robert A Heinlein)
Flight Of The Raven (by Stephanie S Tolan)
Flying Dutchman (by Joseph Ward Moore)
Folk of the Fringe, The (by Orson Scott Card)
Fugue for a Darkening Island (by Christopher

Priest)
Fulfilments of Fate and Desire, The (by Storm Constantine)
Full Circle (by Bruce Arris)
Galapagos (by Kurt Vonnegut)
Genocides, The (by Thomas Disch)
Girl Who Owned a City (by O T Nelson)
Giver, The (by Lois Lowry)
Glimmering (by Elizabeth Hand)
God's Grace (by Bernard Malamud)
Greybeard (by Brian W Aldiss)
Guardians (Series) (by Victor Milan aka Richard Austin)
Handmaids Tale, The (by Margaret Atwood)
He, She and It (by Marge Piercy)
Hollow Lands, The (by Michael Moorcock)
Horsclans (Series) (by Robert Adams)
Hospital Ship (by Martin Bay)
Hunger Games (Series) (by Suzanne Collins)
I Am Legend (by Richard Matheson)
Ice People, The (aka La Nuit Des Temps) (by Rene Barjavel)
Ice People, The (by Maggie Gee)
In the Country of Last Things (by Paul Auster)
Iron Dream, The (by Norman Spinrad)
Kamandi, the Last Boy on Earth Omnibus Volume 1-2 (by Jack Kirby)
Kelwin (by Neal Barrett Jnr)
Kraken Awakes, The (aka Out Of The Deeps) (by John Wyndham)
La Nuit Des Temps (aka The Ice People) (by Rene Barjavel)
Last Book In The Universe, The
Last Fourteen, The (by Tyrone Barry)
Last Man, The (by Mary Shelley)
Last Ship, The (by William Brinkley)
Last Wave, The (by Petru Popescu)
Legends from the End of Time (by Michael Moorcock)
Level 7 (by Mordecai Roshwald)
Little Puppy that Could, The (part of Einstein's Monsters collection) (by Martin Amis)
Long Loud Silence, The (by Wilson Tucker)
Long Way Back, The (by Margot Bennet)
Long Winter, The (by John Christopher)
Lot (by Ward Moore)
Lot's Daughter (by Ward Moore)

Lucifers Hammer (by Larry Niven)
Malevil (by Ropert Merle)
Maurai Series (by Poul Anderson)
Mop Up (by Richard Laymon)
Mysic Rebel Series (by Ryder Syvertsen)
Natures End (by James Kunetka and Whitley Strieber)
Neena Gathering (by Valerie Nieman Colander)
Night of the Long Knives (by Fritz Reuter Leiber Jr)
Night of the Triffids (by Simon Clark)
No Blade of Grass (by John Christopher)
Nordenholt's Million (by Alfred Walter Stewart)
Nukes: Four Horror Writers on the Ultimate Horror (ed. John Maclay)
One Second After (by William R Forstchen)
On the Beach (by Nevil Shute)
Oryx And Crake (by Margaret Atwood)
Out of the Deeps (aka The Kraken Awakes) (by John Wyndham)
Outlanders Series (by James Axler)
Overload (Series) (by Bob Hams)
Patriots: Surviving the Coming Collapse (by James W Rawles)
Pendulum (by John Christopher)
Penultimate Truth, The (by Philip K Dick)
Pesthouse, The (Jim Crace)
Phoenix (Series) (by David Alexander)
Place of the Gods (by Stephen Vincent Benet)
Plague (by Graham Masterton)
Plague 99 (by Jean Ure)
Postman, The (by David Brin)
Protectors War, The (by S M Stirling))
Pulling Through (by Dean Ing)
Purple Cloud, The (by M P Shiel)
Ragged Edge, The (by John Christopher)
Ravage (by Rene Barjavel)
Riddley Walker (by Russell Hoban)
Rift, The (by Walter J Williams)
Road, The (Cormac McCarthy)
Saint Leibowitz and the Wild Horse Woman (by Walter Miller)
Scarlet Plague, The (by Jack London)
Second Deluge, The (by Garrett Putman Serviss)
Shades Children (by Garth Nix)

Shadow On The Hearth, The (by Judith
    Merril)
Shore Of Women, The (by Pamela Sargent)
Some Will Not Die (by Algis Budrys)
Stand, The (by Stephen King)
Steel Beach (by John Varley)
Strange Invaders, The (by Alun Llewellyn)
Sun Grows Cold, The (by Howard Berk)
Survivalist (Series) (by Jerry Ahern)
Survivors (by Terry Nation)
Survivors: Genesis of a Hero (by John Eyers)
Swan Song (by Robert R McCammon)
There Will Be War (ed. Jerry Eugene
Pournelle)
Third World War, The (by Sir John Hackett)
This Immortal (by Roger Zelazny)
This Is The Way The World Ends
Thunder and Roses (by Theodore Strugeon)
Through Darkest America (by Neal Barrett
    Jr.)
Tight Little Stitches in a Dead Man's Back
Time Disease, The (part of Einstein's
    Monsters collection) (by Martin Amis)
Tomorrow, When The War Began (Series)
    (by John Marsden)
Toms A-Cold (by John Collier)
Torch, The (by Jack Bechdolt)
Traveler (Series), The (by D B Drumm)
Twilight World (by Poul Anderson)
Vanishing Point (by Michaela Roessner)
Warday (by Whitley Streiber and James
    Kuselka)
Wasteworld (Series) (by James Barton)
Watcher At The Shrine (by Jean Ure)
Welcome To The Ark (by Stephanie S Tolan)
When The Wind Blows (by Raymond Briggs)
When Worlds Collide (by Edwin Balmer &
    Philip Wylie)
Where Late The Sweet Birds Sang (by Kate
    Wilhelm)
White Plague, The (by Frank Herbert)
Wild Shore, The (by Kim Stanley Robinson)
Wind From Nowhere, The (by J G Ballard)
Wingman (Series) (by Mack Maloney)
Winter of the World, The (by Poul Anderson)
World In Winter, The (by John Christopher)
Wolf And Iron (by Gordon R Dickson)
Year Of The Flood, The (by Margaret
    Atwood)

Z for Zachariah (by Robert C O'Brien)

Notes:

Notes:

About the writer...

Andy McClung, the writer of these lessons, was born into a Cumberland Presbyterian family, was baptized as an infant in a CP church, was taught what it means to be a Christian in a CP church, professed his faith in a CP church, and heard the call to ministry in a CP church. When God told Andy that he was supposed to become a minister, though, Andy realized he didn't really know much about the CP church. A few years at Memphis Theological Seminary fixed that. Andy graduated from MTS with a Master of Divinity degree in 1994 and loved learning so much that he went back to earn a Doctor Ministry degree in 2002. He still loves to learn.

Over the years, Andy has served CP congregations in Alabama, Mississippi, and Tennessee as youth minister, stated supply, associate pastor, church administrator, interim pastor, and pastor. He has served as interim pastor and pulpit supply in churches of other denominations too, but he's never been tempted to leave the CP Church. Not only is it home for him, but - more importantly - the CP Church has the best theology out there.

Nowadays Andy lives in Memphis, Tennessee. He writes for fun and a little bit of profit (though he hopes to write for much more profit some day); preaches on Sundays; and serves as a part-time professor at MTS, teaching the Cumberland Presbyterian courses. He also serves in a variety of roles on the presbyterial, synodic, and denominational levels. His full-time occupation, though, is being husband to Rev. Tiffany Hall McClung and father to Ian (9) and Maggie (6). His hobbies are many and varied, and probably of interest to no one but himself.

Since teachers usually end up learning far more than they pass along to their students, and since writing curriculum is essentially teaching teachers, Andy is extremely thankful for being asked to write these lessons. It is his sincere prayer that they draw teachers and students closer to God, through Christ, by the power of the Holy Spirit. Additionally, Andy hopes that these lessons strengthen students and teachers in their Cumberland Presbyterianism.

Project editor is Susan Guin Groce. Additional editing by Cindy Martin. Electronic processing and incidental layout by Matthew Gore. Cover photo by Matthew Gore. *Faith Out Loud* logo by Joanna Bellis. Produced for the Discipleship Ministry Team of the Ministry Council of the Cumberland Presbyterian Church.

Faith Out Loud!
New Cumberland Presbyterian curriculum for youth!

Each **Faith Out Loud** volume includes 13 reproducible weekly lessons for youth providing your church with all the material they need for an entire quarter. Written by Cumberland Presbyterians for Cumberland Presbyterians, lessons can be purchased in attractive volumes or download singly or in quarters. **$55 a Quarter or $210 Full Year (download or hardcopy).**

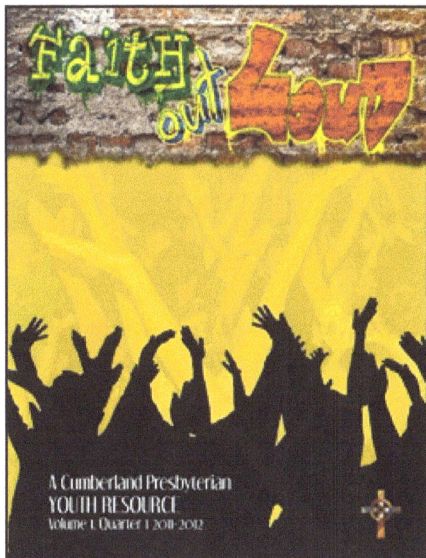

Faith Out Loud - Volume 1

We are excited to release this curriculum to equip you to guide and educate your students towards a deeper faith in Christ and a growing understanding of the beliefs we hold as Cumberland Presbyterians. The series author, Dr. Andy McClung, has created engaging lessons that help students begin to think deeply and critically about their Christian beliefs and offers them practical ways to live out their faith daily.

It is our prayer that these lessons both encourage you and equip you as a youth leader—we're so grateful for what you do in the lives of students!

Each lesson includes:

Lesson Title: Each lesson has a catchy title. Use these titles as teasers to get your students excited about upcoming gatherings.

Scripture: Each lesson has a key scripture reference. Spend some time studying and praying through each week's passage as you prepare to teach.

Theme: The theme statement gives you a quick snapshot into the main point of the lesson.

Before The Lesson: This section is usually divided into two parts: *Supplies* and *Preparations*. *Supplies* give you a quick list of all the stuff you need to gather for each week. *Preparations* give detailed instructions on the advance work that needs to be done for that week's activities. Do NOT wait until the night before you teach to review this section.

The Lesson: Once you move into the teaching time, you'll see these recurring elements:

✔**Opening Activity:** These activities are designed to draw students into the material and set up the theme for the lesson.

✔**Discussion Questions:** Usually a group of open-ended questions, these moments in the lesson are strategically placed to encourage your students to both think about and respond to the topic at hand.

✔**Explain:** Placed in *italics*, these sections can be read verbatim to your students to help them fully understand the implications of the topic or theme. You'll discover you'll get the best response when you are thoroughly familiar with these sections and can deliver the same information in your own words instead of just reading the info to the students.

✔**Leader Notes:** You'll find sections of blue text throughout each lesson (gray in printed copies). These are notes just for you, the leader. These notes offer you everything from instructions on how to facilitate the activities to background information on the subject to tips in making your lesson run smoothly.

✔**Read:** This section highlights a key scripture passage that should be read aloud. Encourage student to do these readings as often as possible.

✔**Parting Ways:** This is simply just the closing of each lesson, designed to help you end your time with your students well and offer them something to think about in the week ahead. Most weeks have handouts to pass along to your students during this time. You may find it helpful to encourage your students to get a folder to keep these handouts together so they can easily refer to them during the week.

Just In Case: Found after the teaching portion of the lesson, this section offers you as the leader some additional insights into related topics your students may bring up or enrichment that can enhance your understanding of the material.

Handouts: At the end of each week's lesson, you'll find a reproducible page. Your purchase of this curriculum grants you the right to print and distribute copies to everyone in your group.

Faith Out Loud is intended for group study in the quarter system but each piece can be used at the discretion of the user. Individual lessons can be purchased online making Faith Out Loud an entirely customizable.

Order from Cumberland Presbyterian Resources, (901) 276-4581 or resources@cumberland.org

Sermons and Papers: A Snapshot of the Year 2010 in the Cumberland Presbyterian Church

Compiled and edited by Dr. Andy McClung. Historical Foundation, 2011. Trade paperback, 121 pages. $19.95.

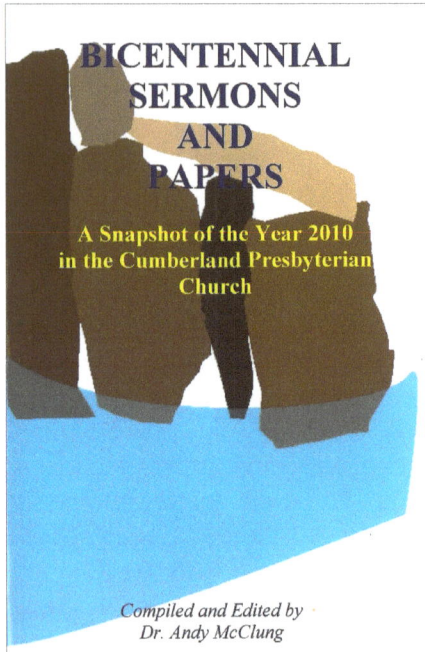

BICENTENNIAL SERMONS AND PAPERS

A Snapshot of the Year 2010 in the Cumberland Presbyterian Church

Compiled and Edited by Dr. Andy McClung

Bicentennial Sermons & Papers

In 1910, R.L. Baskette published a book which compiled sermons preached to and papers delivered before the delegates and guests that same year at the meeting of General Assembly in Dickson, Tennessee. The book, titled Centennial Sermons and Papers, celebrated the one hundredth birthday of the Cumberland Presbyterian Church. Inspired by Mr. Baskette's work, the book you now read contains a collection of sermons and papers as well. The majority of these sermons and papers, however, were not presented at the 2010 meeting of General Assembly (which was again in Dickson, Tennessee). Rather, the sermons were preached by Cumberland Presbyterians to Cumberland Presbyterians in various settings across the United States during 2010, our bicentennial year. It is my hope that this book will preserve a snapshot of what Cumberland Presbyterians were hearing from Cumberland Presbyterian pulpits during this historic year of our bicentennial.

Contributors include:

Melissa Malinoski, Pat Pottorff, J. David Hester, Brent Wills, Scott Yates, Barney Hudson, Jennifer Hayes, Mark Allison, Pam Phillips Burk, Roy Hall, T. J. Malinoski, Chris Warren, William Warren, Daniel Barkley, Stewart P. Salyer, Aaron M. Ferry, Marcus Hayes, and Patrick Wilkerson.

Shall Woman Preach? Or the Question Answered

by Rev. Louisa M. Woosley. One of the most important pieces of Cumberland Presbyterian literature. This Kentuckian was the first woman ordained to the ministry in all of the Reformed tradition. Shortly after her ordination by Nolin Presbytery in 1889, Louisa wrote this volume to justify her call to a skeptical church. Trade Paperback, $8.95.

A Brief History of Cumberland College 1825-1861

by Matthew H. Gore, trade paperback, 2010, $19.95. Located in Princeton, Kentucky, Cumberland College was the denominations first attempt at an institution of higher education. Although the institution was plagued by financial problems many early prominent Cumberland Presbyterians were educated at Cumberland College. This volume also includes an expanded roll of all known students with their date of graduation when known.

The Boys Who Went To War from Cumberland University, 1861-1865

by William Floyd & Paul Gibson. Thomas Publications, 2002. Hardcover, 208 pages, photo illustrated, $24.95. This book is a compilation of two original autograph books, with photos, from Cumberland University in Lebanon, Tennessee. The photos and capsule biographies present a fascinating story of over 150 students and faculty. Many of "the boys" joined the 7th Tennessee Infantry. A unique piece of Tennessee history. Prior to 1906, Cumberland University was the flagship educational institution of the Cumberland Presbyterian Church.

This They Believed: A Brief History of Doctrine in the Cumberland Presbyterian Church

by Joe Ben Irby. Hardcover, 764 pages, Historical Foundation, 2009 edition, $36.95. This massive volume presents an overview of Cumberland Presbyterian theology. Irby was professor emeritus of theology at Memphis Theological Seminary.

Order from Cumberland Presbyterian Resources, (901) 276-4581 or resources@cumberland.org

www.ingramcontent.com/pod-product-compliance
Lightning Source LLC
Chambersburg PA
CBHW041224040426
42443CB00002B/79